# 50 Ultimate Winter Dishes for Home

By: Kelly Johnson

# Table of Contents

- Beef Stew
- Chicken Pot Pie
- Roasted Butternut Squash Soup
- Lasagna
- Pot Roast
- Baked Mac and Cheese
- Chili
- Creamy Tomato Soup
- Shepherd's Pie
- Baked Ziti
- Chicken and Dumplings
- Beef Wellington
- Roasted Root Vegetables
- Short Ribs
- Chicken Alfredo
- French Onion Soup
- Spaghetti Bolognese
- Pulled Pork Sandwiches
- Sweet Potato Casserole
- Meatloaf
- Roasted Brussels Sprouts
- Stuffed Bell Peppers
- Beef and Barley Soup
- Beef and Potato Stew
- Sausage and Kale Soup
- Roasted Chicken with Vegetables
- Stuffed Mushrooms
- Potato Leek Soup
- Chicken Enchiladas
- Beef Empanadas
- Chicken Parmesan
- Risotto with Mushrooms
- Fettuccine Alfredo
- Baked Sweet Potatoes
- Cranberry Sauce
- Meatball Subs

- Chicken Marsala
- Clam Chowder
- Turkey Tetrazzini
- Spinach and Ricotta Stuffed Shells
- Pumpkin Ravioli
- Braised Lamb Shanks
- Eggplant Parmesan
- Roast Pork Loin
- Sweet and Sour Meatballs
- Braised Chicken with Root Vegetables
- Roasted Carrots with Honey
- Pecan Pie
- Apple Crisp
- Hot Cocoa with Marshmallows

# Beef Stew

## Ingredients:

- 1 lb beef stew meat, cubed
- 2 tbsp olive oil
- 1 onion, chopped
- 2 garlic cloves, minced
- 3 carrots, sliced
- 3 potatoes, peeled and cubed
- 2 cups beef broth
- 1 cup red wine
- 1 tbsp tomato paste
- 1 tsp dried thyme
- 1 bay leaf
- Salt and pepper to taste
- Fresh parsley for garnish

## Instructions:

1. In a large pot, heat olive oil over medium heat. Brown the beef cubes on all sides, then remove and set aside.
2. In the same pot, add the onion and garlic and cook for 3 minutes until softened.
3. Stir in the tomato paste and cook for another minute.
4. Add the beef broth, red wine, thyme, and bay leaf. Bring to a boil.
5. Return the beef to the pot along with the carrots and potatoes. Season with salt and pepper.
6. Reduce the heat and simmer, covered, for 1.5-2 hours, until the beef is tender.
7. Discard the bay leaf, garnish with fresh parsley, and serve.

# Chicken Pot Pie

**Ingredients:**

- 2 cups cooked chicken, diced
- 1 cup frozen peas and carrots
- 1/2 cup onion, chopped
- 1/4 cup butter
- 1/4 cup all-purpose flour
- 2 cups chicken broth
- 1 cup milk
- Salt and pepper to taste
- 2 refrigerated pie crusts

**Instructions:**

1. Preheat your oven to 425°F (220°C).
2. In a large pan, melt butter over medium heat. Add the onion and cook for 5 minutes.
3. Stir in the flour and cook for 1 minute. Slowly add the chicken broth and milk, whisking until smooth.
4. Add the chicken and peas and carrots. Season with salt and pepper. Cook until the mixture thickens.
5. Roll out one pie crust and fit it into a pie dish. Pour the chicken mixture into the pie.
6. Cover with the second pie crust, crimping the edges. Cut slits in the top for steam to escape.
7. Bake for 30-35 minutes, or until the crust is golden brown. Let cool for 10 minutes before serving.

# Roasted Butternut Squash Soup

## Ingredients:

- 1 medium butternut squash, peeled and cubed
- 1 onion, chopped
- 2 garlic cloves, minced
- 4 cups vegetable broth
- 1 cup coconut milk
- 1 tbsp olive oil
- 1 tsp ground cumin
- Salt and pepper to taste
- Fresh parsley for garnish

## Instructions:

1. Preheat the oven to 400°F (200°C).
2. Toss the butternut squash cubes with olive oil, cumin, salt, and pepper. Roast on a baking sheet for 25-30 minutes, until tender.
3. In a large pot, sauté the onion and garlic over medium heat for 5 minutes until softened.
4. Add the roasted squash and vegetable broth to the pot. Bring to a simmer and cook for 10 minutes.
5. Use an immersion blender to blend the soup until smooth, or transfer it to a blender in batches.
6. Stir in the coconut milk and heat for 5 minutes.
7. Garnish with fresh parsley and serve.

# Lasagna

### Ingredients:

- 1 lb ground beef
- 1 onion, chopped
- 2 garlic cloves, minced
- 1 can (28 oz) crushed tomatoes
- 1 can (6 oz) tomato paste
- 1 tbsp sugar
- 1 tsp dried basil
- 1 tsp dried oregano
- Salt and pepper to taste
- 12 lasagna noodles, cooked
- 2 cups ricotta cheese
- 1 egg
- 2 cups shredded mozzarella cheese
- 1 cup grated Parmesan cheese

### Instructions:

1. Preheat your oven to 375°F (190°C).
2. In a large pan, brown the ground beef over medium heat with the onion and garlic. Drain excess fat.
3. Stir in the crushed tomatoes, tomato paste, sugar, basil, oregano, salt, and pepper. Simmer for 15 minutes.
4. In a separate bowl, mix the ricotta cheese with the egg.
5. In a baking dish, spread a thin layer of meat sauce, then layer with cooked lasagna noodles, ricotta mixture, mozzarella, and Parmesan. Repeat layers, finishing with a layer of sauce and mozzarella.
6. Cover with foil and bake for 30 minutes. Remove the foil and bake for an additional 10 minutes, until bubbly and golden.
7. Let rest for 10 minutes before serving.

## Pot Roast

**Ingredients:**

- 3 lb beef chuck roast
- 2 tbsp olive oil
- 1 onion, chopped
- 2 garlic cloves, minced
- 4 cups beef broth
- 1 tbsp Worcestershire sauce
- 1 tbsp tomato paste
- 4 carrots, peeled and cut into chunks
- 4 potatoes, peeled and cut into chunks
- Salt and pepper to taste
- Fresh thyme for garnish

**Instructions:**

1. Preheat your oven to 325°F (165°C).
2. Heat olive oil in a large oven-safe pot over medium-high heat. Brown the roast on all sides, then remove and set aside.
3. In the same pot, sauté the onion and garlic until softened.
4. Stir in the beef broth, Worcestershire sauce, and tomato paste. Return the roast to the pot and add the carrots and potatoes.
5. Cover and roast for 3-4 hours, or until the beef is tender.
6. Remove the roast and vegetables, slice, and serve with the pan juices. Garnish with fresh thyme.

## Baked Mac and Cheese

**Ingredients:**

- 8 oz elbow macaroni
- 2 cups shredded cheddar cheese
- 1 cup milk
- 1/4 cup butter
- 2 tbsp flour
- 1 tsp mustard powder
- 1/2 tsp garlic powder
- Salt and pepper to taste
- 1/2 cup breadcrumbs

**Instructions:**

1. Preheat your oven to 350°F (175°C).
2. Cook the macaroni according to package instructions, then drain.
3. In a pot, melt butter over medium heat. Stir in the flour, mustard powder, garlic powder, salt, and pepper, and cook for 1-2 minutes.
4. Gradually whisk in the milk and cook until thickened. Stir in 1 1/2 cups of shredded cheese until melted and smooth.
5. Mix the cooked pasta with the cheese sauce, then pour into a greased baking dish.
6. Top with breadcrumbs and the remaining cheese.
7. Bake for 25-30 minutes, until bubbly and golden brown.

## Chili

**Ingredients:**

- 1 lb ground beef
- 1 onion, chopped
- 2 garlic cloves, minced
- 2 cans (14.5 oz each) diced tomatoes
- 1 can (6 oz) tomato paste
- 1 can (15 oz) kidney beans, drained and rinsed
- 1 can (15 oz) black beans, drained and rinsed
- 1 tbsp chili powder
- 1 tsp cumin
- Salt and pepper to taste

**Instructions:**

1. In a large pot, brown the ground beef over medium heat with the onion and garlic.
2. Stir in the diced tomatoes, tomato paste, beans, chili powder, cumin, salt, and pepper.
3. Bring to a simmer and cook for 30 minutes, stirring occasionally.
4. Adjust seasoning as needed and serve hot with toppings such as sour cream, cheese, and jalapeños.

# Creamy Tomato Soup

## Ingredients:

- 2 tbsp butter
- 1 onion, chopped
- 2 garlic cloves, minced
- 2 cans (14.5 oz each) diced tomatoes
- 1 cup vegetable broth
- 1/2 cup heavy cream
- Salt and pepper to taste
- Fresh basil for garnish

## Instructions:

1. In a pot, melt butter over medium heat. Add the onion and garlic and sauté until softened.
2. Stir in the diced tomatoes and vegetable broth. Bring to a boil, then reduce heat and simmer for 15 minutes.
3. Use an immersion blender to blend the soup until smooth, or transfer to a blender in batches.
4. Stir in the heavy cream, and season with salt and pepper.
5. Garnish with fresh basil and serve hot with grilled cheese.

## Shepherd's Pie

**Ingredients:**

- 1 lb ground lamb or beef
- 1 onion, chopped
- 2 carrots, diced
- 1 cup peas
- 1 cup beef broth
- 1 tbsp tomato paste
- 1 tbsp Worcestershire sauce
- 4 cups mashed potatoes
- Salt and pepper to taste

**Instructions:**

1. Preheat your oven to 375°F (190°C).
2. Brown the ground meat in a pan, then add the onion and carrots. Cook for 5 minutes until softened.
3. Stir in the peas, beef broth, tomato paste, Worcestershire sauce, salt, and pepper. Simmer for 10 minutes.
4. Transfer the meat mixture to a baking dish, then top with mashed potatoes.
5. Bake for 20 minutes, until the potatoes are golden brown. Serve hot.

## Baked Ziti

### Ingredients:

- 12 oz ziti pasta
- 1 jar (24 oz) marinara sauce
- 2 cups ricotta cheese
- 2 cups shredded mozzarella cheese
- 1/2 cup grated Parmesan cheese
- 1 tsp dried basil
- Salt and pepper to taste

### Instructions:

1. Preheat your oven to 375°F (190°C).
2. Cook the ziti pasta according to package instructions, then drain.
3. In a large bowl, mix the pasta with marinara sauce, ricotta, 1 cup mozzarella, Parmesan, basil, salt, and pepper.
4. Pour into a baking dish and top with the remaining mozzarella.
5. Bake for 25-30 minutes, until bubbly and golden brown.

## Chicken and Dumplings

**Ingredients:**

- 2 cups cooked chicken, shredded
- 4 cups chicken broth
- 1 cup carrots, sliced
- 1 cup celery, diced
- 1 onion, chopped
- 2 cups all-purpose flour
- 1/2 cup milk
- 1 tsp baking powder
- 1/2 tsp salt
- 2 tbsp butter

**Instructions:**

1. In a large pot, combine the chicken broth, carrots, celery, and onion. Bring to a simmer and cook for 10 minutes.
2. Add the shredded chicken and cook for 5 minutes.
3. In a bowl, combine the flour, milk, baking powder, salt, and butter to make a dough.
4. Drop spoonfuls of dough into the soup and simmer for 10-12 minutes, until the dumplings are cooked through.
5. Serve hot with extra parsley for garnish.

# Beef Wellington

## Ingredients:

- 1.5 lb beef tenderloin
- 2 tbsp olive oil
- Salt and pepper to taste
- 1/2 cup Dijon mustard
- 8 oz cremini mushrooms, finely chopped
- 1/2 cup pâté (optional)
- 1 package puff pastry (enough to wrap the beef)
- 1 egg, beaten for egg wash

## Instructions:

1. Preheat your oven to 400°F (200°C).
2. Sear the beef tenderloin in a hot pan with olive oil for 2-3 minutes on all sides. Season with salt and pepper. Once seared, brush with Dijon mustard and let cool.
3. Sauté the mushrooms in a pan until all moisture evaporates. Let them cool.
4. Roll out the puff pastry on a floured surface. Spread a thin layer of pâté (if using) on the pastry. Place the beef in the center and top with the mushroom mixture.
5. Carefully fold the pastry over the beef, sealing the edges. Brush with beaten egg.
6. Bake for 25-30 minutes, until the pastry is golden brown. Let rest for 10 minutes before slicing and serving.

# Roasted Root Vegetables

## Ingredients:

- 2 carrots, peeled and sliced
- 2 parsnips, peeled and sliced
- 2 sweet potatoes, peeled and cubed
- 1 onion, chopped
- 2 tbsp olive oil
- 1 tsp thyme
- Salt and pepper to taste

## Instructions:

1. Preheat your oven to 425°F (220°C).
2. Toss the vegetables with olive oil, thyme, salt, and pepper.
3. Spread them out on a baking sheet in a single layer.
4. Roast for 30-35 minutes, stirring halfway through, until tender and lightly caramelized.

# Short Ribs

**Ingredients:**

- 4 bone-in beef short ribs
- 2 tbsp olive oil
- Salt and pepper to taste
- 1 onion, chopped
- 2 carrots, peeled and chopped
- 2 celery stalks, chopped
- 3 garlic cloves, minced
- 1 cup red wine
- 3 cups beef broth
- 1 tbsp tomato paste
- 2 sprigs fresh thyme
- 2 sprigs fresh rosemary

**Instructions:**

1. Preheat the oven to 325°F (165°C).
2. Heat olive oil in a large Dutch oven over medium-high heat. Brown the short ribs on all sides, seasoning with salt and pepper. Remove and set aside.
3. In the same pot, sauté the onion, carrots, and celery for 5-7 minutes. Add the garlic and cook for another minute.
4. Stir in the tomato paste and cook for 2 minutes. Add the wine and cook for 5 minutes to reduce slightly.
5. Return the ribs to the pot, add the beef broth, thyme, and rosemary. Bring to a simmer.
6. Cover the pot and transfer it to the oven. Cook for 2.5-3 hours, until the ribs are tender.
7. Serve the ribs with the braising liquid and vegetables.

## Chicken Alfredo

### Ingredients:

- 1 lb chicken breasts, boneless and skinless
- 2 tbsp olive oil
- Salt and pepper to taste
- 12 oz fettuccine pasta
- 3/4 cup heavy cream
- 1 cup grated Parmesan cheese
- 2 tbsp butter
- 1 garlic clove, minced
- Fresh parsley for garnish

### Instructions:

1. Cook the fettuccine according to package instructions. Drain and set aside.
2. Season the chicken breasts with salt and pepper. Heat olive oil in a skillet over medium heat. Cook the chicken for 6-7 minutes per side, until cooked through. Slice the chicken.
3. In a large skillet, melt the butter over medium heat. Add the garlic and cook for 1 minute.
4. Pour in the cream and bring to a simmer. Stir in the Parmesan cheese and cook until the sauce thickens.
5. Toss the cooked pasta in the sauce. Add the sliced chicken on top and garnish with parsley.

# French Onion Soup

## Ingredients:

- 4 large onions, thinly sliced
- 2 tbsp butter
- 1 tbsp olive oil
- 2 garlic cloves, minced
- 1 tsp thyme
- 4 cups beef broth
- 1 cup white wine
- 1 bay leaf
- 1 tbsp flour
- 1 baguette, sliced
- 1 cup shredded Gruyère cheese

## Instructions:

1. In a large pot, melt the butter and olive oil over medium heat. Add the onions and cook, stirring occasionally, for 30-35 minutes, until caramelized.
2. Add the garlic and thyme, and cook for another minute.
3. Stir in the flour and cook for 2 minutes.
4. Add the wine, scraping up any brown bits from the bottom of the pot. Stir in the beef broth and bay leaf. Bring to a simmer and cook for 15-20 minutes.
5. Preheat your broiler. Ladle the soup into oven-safe bowls, top with baguette slices, and sprinkle with cheese.
6. Broil for 2-3 minutes, until the cheese is melted and bubbly. Serve hot.

## Spaghetti Bolognese

### Ingredients:

- 1 lb ground beef or pork
- 1 onion, chopped
- 2 garlic cloves, minced
- 1 carrot, grated
- 1 celery stalk, chopped
- 1 can (28 oz) crushed tomatoes
- 1 tbsp tomato paste
- 1 tsp dried oregano
- 1 tsp dried basil
- 1/4 cup red wine
- 1 lb spaghetti
- Salt and pepper to taste
- Fresh basil for garnish

### Instructions:

1. In a large pan, cook the ground meat over medium heat until browned. Remove excess fat.
2. Add the onion, garlic, carrot, and celery, and cook for 5-7 minutes, until softened.
3. Stir in the tomato paste and cook for 1-2 minutes. Add the crushed tomatoes, oregano, basil, red wine, salt, and pepper.
4. Simmer the sauce for 30 minutes, stirring occasionally.
5. Cook the spaghetti according to package instructions. Drain and toss with the Bolognese sauce.
6. Garnish with fresh basil and serve.

# Pulled Pork Sandwiches

## Ingredients:

- 3 lb pork shoulder
- 2 tbsp olive oil
- Salt and pepper to taste
- 1 onion, chopped
- 2 garlic cloves, minced
- 1 cup barbecue sauce
- 1/2 cup apple cider vinegar
- 1 tbsp brown sugar
- 1 tsp smoked paprika
- 8 sandwich buns
- Coleslaw for topping (optional)

## Instructions:

1. Preheat your oven to 300°F (150°C).
2. Rub the pork shoulder with olive oil, salt, and pepper. Sear the pork in a hot skillet for 3-4 minutes on each side, then transfer to a roasting pan.
3. Add the onion, garlic, barbecue sauce, apple cider vinegar, brown sugar, and paprika to the pan. Cover with foil.
4. Roast for 3-4 hours, until the pork is tender and easily shredded.
5. Shred the pork with two forks and mix it with the sauce in the pan.
6. Serve the pulled pork on sandwich buns, topped with coleslaw.

## Sweet Potato Casserole

### Ingredients:

- 4 large sweet potatoes, peeled and cubed
- 1/4 cup butter
- 1/2 cup brown sugar
- 1/4 cup milk
- 1 tsp vanilla extract
- 1/2 tsp cinnamon
- 1/2 cup mini marshmallows

### Instructions:

1. Preheat your oven to 375°F (190°C).
2. Boil the sweet potatoes in salted water until tender, about 15-20 minutes. Drain and mash.
3. Stir in butter, brown sugar, milk, vanilla, and cinnamon.
4. Transfer the mashed sweet potatoes to a baking dish and top with mini marshmallows.
5. Bake for 20 minutes, or until the marshmallows are golden brown.

# Meatloaf

## Ingredients:

- 1 lb ground beef
- 1/2 lb ground pork
- 1 onion, chopped
- 2 garlic cloves, minced
- 1 cup breadcrumbs
- 1/4 cup milk
- 1 egg
- 1/4 cup ketchup
- 1 tbsp Worcestershire sauce
- Salt and pepper to taste
- 1/4 cup ketchup for topping

## Instructions:

1. Preheat your oven to 350°F (175°C).
2. In a bowl, mix the beef, pork, onion, garlic, breadcrumbs, milk, egg, ketchup, Worcestershire sauce, salt, and pepper.
3. Transfer the mixture to a loaf pan and shape into a loaf.
4. Spread ketchup on top of the loaf.
5. Bake for 1 hour, until the meatloaf is cooked through. Let rest for 10 minutes before slicing.

# Roasted Brussels Sprouts

## Ingredients:

- 1 lb Brussels sprouts, trimmed and halved
- 2 tbsp olive oil
- Salt and pepper to taste
- 1 tbsp balsamic vinegar (optional)

## Instructions:

1. Preheat your oven to 400°F (200°C).
2. Toss the Brussels sprouts with olive oil, salt, and pepper.
3. Spread them on a baking sheet in a single layer.
4. Roast for 20-25 minutes, stirring halfway through, until crispy and golden.
5. Drizzle with balsamic vinegar before serving (optional).

# Stuffed Bell Peppers

## Ingredients:

- 4 bell peppers, tops cut off and seeds removed
- 1 lb ground beef or turkey
- 1 onion, chopped
- 2 cloves garlic, minced
- 1 cup cooked rice
- 1 can (14 oz) diced tomatoes
- 1 tbsp tomato paste
- 1 tsp dried oregano
- 1 tsp dried basil
- Salt and pepper to taste
- 1 cup shredded cheese (optional)

## Instructions:

1. Preheat your oven to 375°F (190°C).
2. In a skillet, cook the ground beef or turkey with onion and garlic over medium heat until browned.
3. Stir in the cooked rice, diced tomatoes, tomato paste, oregano, basil, salt, and pepper. Simmer for 5-7 minutes.
4. Stuff the peppers with the mixture and place them in a baking dish.
5. Cover with foil and bake for 30 minutes. If desired, top with cheese and bake uncovered for an additional 5 minutes until the cheese is melted.

# Beef and Barley Soup

## Ingredients:

- 1 lb beef stew meat, cut into cubes
- 2 tbsp olive oil
- 1 onion, chopped
- 2 carrots, peeled and sliced
- 2 celery stalks, chopped
- 2 garlic cloves, minced
- 1 cup pearl barley
- 6 cups beef broth
- 1 tsp dried thyme
- Salt and pepper to taste
- 1 bay leaf

## Instructions:

1. In a large pot, heat olive oil over medium-high heat. Brown the beef cubes on all sides, then remove and set aside.
2. In the same pot, add the onion, carrots, celery, and garlic. Cook for 5-7 minutes until softened.
3. Add the barley, beef broth, thyme, salt, pepper, and bay leaf. Bring to a boil.
4. Reduce the heat and simmer for 1-1.5 hours, until the beef and barley are tender.
5. Remove the bay leaf and serve hot.

# Beef and Potato Stew

## Ingredients:

- 1 lb beef stew meat, cut into cubes
- 2 tbsp olive oil
- 1 onion, chopped
- 2 carrots, peeled and chopped
- 2 potatoes, peeled and cubed
- 3 cups beef broth
- 1 tsp dried thyme
- 1/2 tsp smoked paprika
- Salt and pepper to taste
- 1 bay leaf

## Instructions:

1. In a large pot, heat olive oil over medium-high heat. Brown the beef cubes on all sides, then remove and set aside.
2. In the same pot, add the onion and carrots, cooking for 5-7 minutes until softened.
3. Add the potatoes, beef broth, thyme, paprika, salt, pepper, and bay leaf. Bring to a boil.
4. Reduce the heat and simmer for 1-1.5 hours, until the beef and potatoes are tender.
5. Remove the bay leaf and serve hot.

## Sausage and Kale Soup

### Ingredients:

- 1 lb Italian sausage, casing removed
- 1 onion, chopped
- 2 cloves garlic, minced
- 6 cups chicken broth
- 1 bunch kale, stems removed and chopped
- 2 medium potatoes, peeled and diced
- 1 tsp dried thyme
- Salt and pepper to taste

### Instructions:

1. In a large pot, cook the sausage over medium heat, breaking it up as it cooks. Once browned, remove and set aside.
2. In the same pot, add the onion and garlic. Cook for 5 minutes until softened.
3. Add the chicken broth, kale, potatoes, thyme, salt, and pepper. Bring to a boil.
4. Reduce the heat and simmer for 30-40 minutes, until the potatoes are tender.
5. Stir the sausage back into the soup and serve hot.

# Roasted Chicken with Vegetables

## Ingredients:

- 1 whole chicken (about 4 lbs)
- 2 tbsp olive oil
- Salt and pepper to taste
- 1 lemon, quartered
- 4 garlic cloves, smashed
- 1 bunch rosemary
- 4 carrots, peeled and cut into chunks
- 2 potatoes, peeled and cut into chunks
- 1 onion, quartered

## Instructions:

1. Preheat your oven to 425°F (220°C).
2. Rub the chicken with olive oil, salt, and pepper. Stuff the cavity with lemon, garlic, and rosemary.
3. Place the chicken in a roasting pan and surround it with the vegetables.
4. Roast for 1.5-2 hours, until the internal temperature reaches 165°F (75°C) and the skin is golden brown.
5. Let the chicken rest for 10 minutes before carving. Serve with the roasted vegetables.

## Stuffed Mushrooms

### Ingredients:

- 12 large mushrooms, stems removed
- 1/2 cup cream cheese, softened
- 1/4 cup grated Parmesan cheese
- 2 tbsp breadcrumbs
- 2 tbsp parsley, chopped
- 1/2 tsp garlic powder
- Salt and pepper to taste

### Instructions:

1. Preheat your oven to 375°F (190°C).
2. In a bowl, mix the cream cheese, Parmesan cheese, breadcrumbs, parsley, garlic powder, salt, and pepper.
3. Stuff the mushroom caps with the mixture and place them on a baking sheet.
4. Bake for 20-25 minutes, until the mushrooms are tender and the filling is golden.
5. Serve warm.

## Potato Leek Soup

### Ingredients:

- 3 large leeks, cleaned and sliced
- 2 tbsp butter
- 4 medium potatoes, peeled and diced
- 4 cups vegetable or chicken broth
- 1 cup heavy cream
- Salt and pepper to taste
- Fresh chives for garnish

### Instructions:

1. In a large pot, melt butter over medium heat. Add the leeks and cook for 5-7 minutes until softened.
2. Add the potatoes and broth. Bring to a boil.
3. Reduce the heat and simmer for 20-25 minutes, until the potatoes are tender.
4. Use an immersion blender or regular blender to puree the soup until smooth.
5. Stir in the heavy cream, salt, and pepper. Garnish with chives and serve.

## Chicken Enchiladas

### Ingredients:

- 4 chicken breasts, cooked and shredded
- 2 cups enchilada sauce
- 1 cup shredded cheese
- 8 corn tortillas
- 1/2 onion, chopped
- 1 tsp cumin
- 1 tsp chili powder
- Salt to taste
- Fresh cilantro for garnish

### Instructions:

1. Preheat your oven to 375°F (190°C).
2. In a bowl, mix the shredded chicken with 1 cup of enchilada sauce, cumin, chili powder, onion, and salt.
3. Heat the tortillas in a dry skillet for a few seconds on each side to soften them.
4. Spread a small amount of enchilada sauce in a baking dish.
5. Fill each tortilla with the chicken mixture and roll it up. Place seam-side down in the dish.
6. Pour the remaining enchilada sauce over the top and sprinkle with cheese.
7. Bake for 20-25 minutes, until the cheese is melted and bubbly.
8. Garnish with cilantro and serve.

# Beef Empanadas

## Ingredients:

- 1 lb ground beef
- 1 onion, chopped
- 1/2 cup olives, chopped
- 1/2 cup raisins
- 1 tsp cumin
- 1 tsp paprika
- 1 package empanada dough discs
- 1 egg, beaten (for egg wash)
- Salt and pepper to taste

## Instructions:

1. In a skillet, cook the ground beef over medium heat until browned.
2. Add the onion, olives, raisins, cumin, paprika, salt, and pepper. Cook for 5-7 minutes until the onion softens.
3. Preheat the oven to 375°F (190°C).
4. Place a spoonful of the beef mixture on each empanada disc. Fold the dough over and press the edges to seal.
5. Brush with the beaten egg and place the empanadas on a baking sheet.
6. Bake for 20-25 minutes, until golden brown. Serve hot.

## Chicken Parmesan

### Ingredients:

- 4 chicken breasts, boneless and skinless
- 1 cup breadcrumbs
- 1/2 cup grated Parmesan cheese
- 1 egg, beaten
- 1 cup marinara sauce
- 1 cup mozzarella cheese, shredded
- Olive oil for frying
- Fresh basil for garnish
- Salt and pepper to taste

### Instructions:

1. Preheat your oven to 375°F (190°C).
2. Season the chicken breasts with salt and pepper.
3. In a shallow bowl, mix the breadcrumbs and Parmesan cheese. Dip the chicken breasts in the beaten egg, then coat them in the breadcrumb mixture.
4. Heat olive oil in a skillet over medium heat. Fry the chicken for 3-4 minutes per side, until golden brown.
5. Place the fried chicken in a baking dish. Top each breast with marinara sauce and mozzarella cheese.
6. Bake for 15-20 minutes, until the chicken is cooked through and the cheese is melted.
7. Garnish with fresh basil and serve.

# Risotto with Mushrooms

## Ingredients:

- 1 cup Arborio rice
- 2 tbsp olive oil
- 1 onion, chopped
- 2 cloves garlic, minced
- 2 cups mushrooms, sliced (cremini, shiitake, or button mushrooms)
- 4 cups chicken or vegetable broth, warmed
- 1/2 cup dry white wine (optional)
- 1/2 cup grated Parmesan cheese
- 1 tbsp butter
- Salt and pepper to taste
- Fresh parsley, chopped (for garnish)

## Instructions:

1. In a large pan, heat olive oil over medium heat. Add the onion and garlic, and cook for 3-4 minutes until softened.
2. Add the mushrooms and cook for another 5-7 minutes, until they release their moisture and become golden.
3. Stir in the rice and cook for 1-2 minutes to lightly toast the rice.
4. If using, pour in the white wine and cook until mostly absorbed.
5. Add the warm broth, one ladleful at a time, stirring constantly and allowing the liquid to absorb before adding more. Continue this process until the rice is tender and creamy (about 18-20 minutes).
6. Stir in the butter, Parmesan cheese, and season with salt and pepper.
7. Serve with a sprinkle of fresh parsley.

## Fettuccine Alfredo

### Ingredients:

- 1 lb fettuccine pasta
- 2 tbsp butter
- 2 cups heavy cream
- 1 cup grated Parmesan cheese
- 2 cloves garlic, minced
- Salt and pepper to taste
- Fresh parsley, chopped (for garnish)

### Instructions:

1. Cook the fettuccine according to the package instructions. Drain and set aside.
2. In a large pan, melt the butter over medium heat. Add the garlic and cook for 1 minute until fragrant.
3. Pour in the heavy cream and bring to a simmer. Cook for 5 minutes, stirring occasionally.
4. Stir in the Parmesan cheese and cook until the sauce thickens, about 3-5 minutes.
5. Add the cooked fettuccine to the pan and toss to coat with the sauce.
6. Season with salt and pepper. Garnish with fresh parsley and serve.

## Baked Sweet Potatoes

### Ingredients:

- 4 medium sweet potatoes
- Olive oil
- Salt and pepper to taste
- Optional toppings: butter, brown sugar, cinnamon, or marshmallows

### Instructions:

1. Preheat the oven to 400°F (200°C).
2. Scrub the sweet potatoes clean and pat them dry.
3. Pierce the sweet potatoes a few times with a fork, then rub them with olive oil and season with salt and pepper.
4. Place the sweet potatoes directly on the oven rack or on a baking sheet.
5. Bake for 45-60 minutes, until tender when pierced with a fork.
6. Serve with your favorite toppings like butter, brown sugar, cinnamon, or marshmallows.

## Cranberry Sauce

### Ingredients:

- 12 oz fresh or frozen cranberries
- 1 cup sugar
- 1/2 cup water
- 1/2 tsp orange zest (optional)
- 1/4 tsp cinnamon (optional)

### Instructions:

1. In a medium saucepan, combine the cranberries, sugar, and water.
2. Bring to a boil, then reduce the heat to a simmer. Cook for 10-15 minutes, stirring occasionally, until the cranberries burst and the sauce thickens.
3. Stir in the orange zest and cinnamon if desired.
4. Remove from heat and let the sauce cool before serving.

# Meatball Subs

## Ingredients:

- 1 lb ground beef or pork
- 1/2 cup breadcrumbs
- 1/4 cup grated Parmesan cheese
- 1 egg
- 2 cloves garlic, minced
- 1 tsp dried oregano
- Salt and pepper to taste
- 2 cups marinara sauce
- 4 sub rolls
- 1 1/2 cups shredded mozzarella cheese

## Instructions:

1. Preheat your oven to 375°F (190°C).
2. In a bowl, combine the ground meat, breadcrumbs, Parmesan, egg, garlic, oregano, salt, and pepper. Form into 12-15 meatballs.
3. Place the meatballs on a baking sheet and bake for 20 minutes, until cooked through.
4. Heat the marinara sauce in a saucepan and add the cooked meatballs. Simmer for 5 minutes.
5. Split the sub rolls and spoon meatballs into each roll. Top with marinara sauce and mozzarella cheese.
6. Place the subs on a baking sheet and bake for 5-7 minutes, until the cheese is melted and bubbly.

## Chicken Marsala

### Ingredients:

- 4 chicken breasts, pounded thin
- 1/2 cup all-purpose flour
- Salt and pepper to taste
- 2 tbsp olive oil
- 8 oz mushrooms, sliced
- 1/2 cup dry Marsala wine
- 1/2 cup chicken broth
- 2 tbsp unsalted butter
- Fresh parsley, chopped (for garnish)

### Instructions:

1. Season the chicken breasts with salt and pepper, then dredge them in flour.
2. Heat olive oil in a large skillet over medium heat. Brown the chicken for 4-5 minutes per side. Remove and set aside.
3. In the same skillet, add the mushrooms and cook for 5 minutes until softened.
4. Add the Marsala wine, chicken broth, and bring to a simmer. Cook for 3-4 minutes to reduce the sauce.
5. Stir in the butter and return the chicken to the skillet. Simmer for another 5-7 minutes, until the chicken is cooked through and the sauce thickens.
6. Garnish with fresh parsley and serve.

# Clam Chowder

## Ingredients:

- 2 cans (6.5 oz) chopped clams, drained
- 2 cups clam juice or chicken broth
- 4 slices bacon, chopped
- 1 onion, chopped
- 2 cloves garlic, minced
- 2 cups potatoes, diced
- 1 cup heavy cream
- 1/2 cup whole milk
- Salt and pepper to taste
- Fresh parsley for garnish

## Instructions:

1. In a large pot, cook the bacon over medium heat until crispy. Remove and set aside.
2. In the same pot, add the onion and garlic. Cook for 5 minutes until softened.
3. Add the potatoes, clam juice, and bring to a boil. Reduce the heat and simmer for 10-15 minutes, until the potatoes are tender.
4. Stir in the clams, heavy cream, and milk. Cook for another 5-7 minutes, until heated through.
5. Season with salt and pepper. Top with bacon and fresh parsley before serving.

# Turkey Tetrazzini

## Ingredients:

- 3 cups cooked turkey, shredded
- 8 oz spaghetti, cooked and drained
- 2 cups mushrooms, sliced
- 1/4 cup butter
- 1/4 cup all-purpose flour
- 2 cups chicken broth
- 1 cup heavy cream
- 1 cup grated Parmesan cheese
- 1/2 tsp garlic powder
- Salt and pepper to taste
- 1/2 cup breadcrumbs

## Instructions:

1. Preheat the oven to 375°F (190°C).
2. In a large pan, melt the butter over medium heat. Add the mushrooms and cook for 5 minutes until softened.
3. Stir in the flour and cook for 2 minutes. Gradually whisk in the chicken broth and cream. Cook until the sauce thickens.
4. Stir in the Parmesan cheese, garlic powder, salt, and pepper.
5. In a baking dish, combine the cooked turkey, spaghetti, and sauce. Top with breadcrumbs.
6. Bake for 25-30 minutes, until bubbly and golden.

# Spinach and Ricotta Stuffed Shells

## Ingredients:

- 12 large pasta shells
- 1 cup ricotta cheese
- 1 cup cooked spinach, squeezed dry and chopped
- 1/2 cup grated Parmesan cheese
- 1 egg
- 1 jar marinara sauce
- 1 cup shredded mozzarella cheese

## Instructions:

1. Preheat the oven to 375°F (190°C).
2. Cook the pasta shells according to package instructions. Drain and set aside.
3. In a bowl, combine the ricotta, spinach, Parmesan, and egg.
4. Stuff the cooked shells with the ricotta mixture and place them in a baking dish.
5. Pour marinara sauce over the stuffed shells and top with mozzarella cheese.
6. Bake for 20-25 minutes, until the cheese is melted and bubbly.

## Pumpkin Ravioli

### Ingredients:

- 1 package fresh or frozen ravioli (pumpkin filling)
- 2 tbsp olive oil
- 2 tbsp butter
- 1/2 tsp sage, dried or fresh
- 1/4 cup Parmesan cheese, grated
- Salt and pepper to taste
- Fresh parsley (for garnish)

### Instructions:

1. Cook the ravioli according to package instructions. Drain and set aside.
2. In a large pan, heat olive oil and butter over medium heat.
3. Add the sage and cook for 1-2 minutes until fragrant.
4. Toss the cooked ravioli in the sage butter sauce.
5. Season with salt and pepper, then sprinkle with Parmesan cheese and garnish with fresh parsley.

# Braised Lamb Shanks

## Ingredients:

- 2 lamb shanks
- 2 tbsp olive oil
- 1 onion, chopped
- 2 carrots, chopped
- 2 celery stalks, chopped
- 4 cloves garlic, minced
- 2 cups red wine
- 2 cups beef broth
- 2 sprigs fresh rosemary
- 1 tsp dried thyme
- Salt and pepper to taste

## Instructions:

1. Preheat the oven to 325°F (165°C).
2. In a large ovenproof pot, heat the olive oil over medium-high heat. Brown the lamb shanks on all sides, then remove and set aside.
3. In the same pot, add the onion, carrots, celery, and garlic. Cook for 5-7 minutes until softened.
4. Add the wine, beef broth, rosemary, thyme, and salt and pepper. Stir to combine.
5. Return the lamb shanks to the pot, cover, and transfer to the oven.
6. Braise for 2-3 hours, until the meat is tender and falling off the bone.
7. Remove the shanks and reduce the sauce on the stove if desired. Serve the lamb with the sauce.

# Eggplant Parmesan

## Ingredients:

- 2 medium eggplants, sliced into 1/2-inch rounds
- Salt (for sweating eggplant)
- 2 cups marinara sauce
- 1 cup grated Parmesan cheese
- 1 cup shredded mozzarella cheese
- 1 cup breadcrumbs
- 1/2 cup all-purpose flour
- 2 eggs, beaten
- 2 tbsp olive oil
- Fresh basil (for garnish)

## Instructions:

1. Preheat the oven to 375°F (190°C).
2. Lay the eggplant slices on paper towels and sprinkle with salt. Let them sit for 30 minutes to draw out excess moisture.
3. Rinse the salt off and pat the slices dry with paper towels.
4. Dredge the eggplant slices in flour, then dip in beaten eggs, and coat in breadcrumbs.
5. In a large skillet, heat olive oil over medium heat and fry the eggplant slices until golden on both sides.
6. In a baking dish, spread a thin layer of marinara sauce. Place a layer of fried eggplant, followed by more sauce and cheeses. Repeat the layers.
7. Bake for 25-30 minutes until bubbly and golden.
8. Garnish with fresh basil before serving.

## Roast Pork Loin

### Ingredients:

- 2 lb pork loin
- 3 cloves garlic, minced
- 2 tbsp olive oil
- 1 tbsp fresh rosemary, chopped
- 1 tbsp fresh thyme, chopped
- 1 tsp salt
- 1/2 tsp pepper
- 1/2 cup white wine or chicken broth

### Instructions:

1. Preheat the oven to 375°F (190°C).
2. Rub the pork loin with garlic, olive oil, rosemary, thyme, salt, and pepper.
3. Place the pork in a roasting pan and roast for 1 hour, or until the internal temperature reaches 145°F (63°C).
4. Halfway through cooking, add the white wine or chicken broth to the pan.
5. Let the pork rest for 10 minutes before slicing.

## Sweet and Sour Meatballs

### Ingredients:

- 1 lb ground beef or pork
- 1/2 cup breadcrumbs
- 1/4 cup milk
- 1 egg
- 1/4 cup grated Parmesan cheese
- 2 cloves garlic, minced
- Salt and pepper to taste
- 1 cup pineapple juice
- 1/2 cup vinegar
- 1/2 cup sugar
- 1 tbsp soy sauce
- 1/4 cup ketchup
- 1/2 cup bell pepper, diced
- 1/2 cup onion, diced

### Instructions:

1. Preheat the oven to 375°F (190°C).
2. In a bowl, mix the ground meat, breadcrumbs, milk, egg, Parmesan, garlic, salt, and pepper.
3. Form into 1-inch meatballs and place them on a baking sheet. Bake for 20-25 minutes until cooked through.
4. In a saucepan, combine pineapple juice, vinegar, sugar, soy sauce, and ketchup. Bring to a simmer.
5. Add the diced bell pepper and onion, cooking for 5-7 minutes.
6. Add the cooked meatballs to the sauce and simmer for 10 minutes. Serve hot.

# Braised Chicken with Root Vegetables

## Ingredients:

- 4 chicken thighs (bone-in)
- 2 tbsp olive oil
- 1 onion, chopped
- 2 carrots, chopped
- 2 parsnips, chopped
- 2 potatoes, chopped
- 4 cloves garlic, minced
- 1 cup chicken broth
- 1 tsp thyme
- Salt and pepper to taste

## Instructions:

1. Preheat the oven to 350°F (175°C).
2. Heat olive oil in a large pot over medium heat. Brown the chicken thighs on both sides, then remove and set aside.
3. In the same pot, sauté the onion, carrots, parsnips, potatoes, and garlic for 5-7 minutes.
4. Add chicken broth, thyme, salt, and pepper, and bring to a simmer.
5. Return the chicken thighs to the pot, cover, and transfer to the oven.
6. Braise for 1 hour, until the chicken is cooked through and the vegetables are tender.

## Roasted Carrots with Honey

### Ingredients:

- 1 lb carrots, peeled and cut into sticks
- 2 tbsp olive oil
- 2 tbsp honey
- Salt and pepper to taste
- Fresh thyme (optional)

### Instructions:

1. Preheat the oven to 400°F (200°C).
2. Toss the carrots with olive oil, honey, salt, and pepper.
3. Arrange on a baking sheet in a single layer.
4. Roast for 25-30 minutes, stirring halfway through, until tender and caramelized.
5. Garnish with fresh thyme if desired.

## Pecan Pie

### Ingredients:

- 1 pie crust (store-bought or homemade)
- 1 cup corn syrup
- 1 cup packed brown sugar
- 1/4 cup butter, melted
- 3 large eggs
- 1 tsp vanilla extract
- 1/2 tsp salt
- 1 1/2 cups pecan halves

### Instructions:

1. Preheat the oven to 350°F (175°C).
2. In a bowl, whisk together the corn syrup, brown sugar, melted butter, eggs, vanilla, and salt.
3. Stir in the pecans.
4. Pour the mixture into the pie crust and spread evenly.
5. Bake for 50-60 minutes until the filling is set and golden. Let cool before serving.

## Apple Crisp

### Ingredients:

- 6 apples, peeled and sliced
- 1 tbsp lemon juice
- 1/2 cup old-fashioned oats
- 1/2 cup flour
- 1/3 cup brown sugar
- 1/4 cup butter, melted
- 1 tsp cinnamon
- Pinch of salt

### Instructions:

1. Preheat the oven to 350°F (175°C).
2. Toss the apple slices with lemon juice and place in a baking dish.
3. In a separate bowl, combine oats, flour, brown sugar, butter, cinnamon, and salt.
4. Sprinkle the oat mixture over the apples.
5. Bake for 40-45 minutes, until the topping is golden and the apples are tender.

# Hot Cocoa with Marshmallows

## Ingredients:

- 2 cups milk
- 2 tbsp cocoa powder
- 2 tbsp sugar
- 1/4 tsp vanilla extract
- Pinch of salt
- Marshmallows for topping

## Instructions:

1. In a saucepan, heat the milk over medium heat.
2. Whisk in the cocoa powder, sugar, vanilla extract, and salt.
3. Heat until the mixture is warm and the sugar is dissolved.
4. Pour into a mug and top with marshmallows.

www.ingramcontent.com/pod-product-compliance
Lightning Source LLC
LaVergne TN
LVHW081506060526
838201LV00056BA/2968